You Can Get Through This
With God's Help

by
Gary Elliott

Dedication

I would like to dedicate this book to God; almost all the poems in this book are from Him and about Him. He is my inspiration, my guide, and the one who loves me, strengthens me, and helps me to get through the good and bad times of my life. My favorite verse in the bible is the first one I memorized, and I have applied it to my life many times.

"Trust in the Lord with all your heart and lean not unto your own understanding; in all your ways acknowledge Him, and He will direct your path."

- *Proverbs 3:5-6*

Acknowledgment

I would like to acknowledge a few people who helped me to write this book. First and foremost, I want to acknowledge my wife, Judy; without her love and support these thirty years, I would be nothing. I have so many friends who have helped me over the years it would take up another 10 pages or more, but I do want to acknowledge Pastor Peter Wilkes, who is with our Heavenly Father now. Without his counseling, I would not have learned so much about myself and God. I want to acknowledge my dear friends who spent a lot of time praying for me: my best friend in High School and life – Ron Kersey (who is also with the Lord). My Tuesday night Catholic bible study group in San Jose, my bible study group in Surprise, AZ, and all the men who were at my bible study group at Lewis prison; Morrey unit (blue side). My dear friends from Mission Bay High School also prayed for me and encouraged me. Thanks to Dennis Yoshonis, who consistently called or texted me almost daily to check on me and encourage me.

Thank you to all the doctors, nurses, and staff (Jessica Acosta-NP) at AZCCC in Surprise, AZ, and the Transplant unit in Scottsdale. Also, the doctor, nurses, and staff at the Research center in Scottsdale. Thank you to Mike and Karen Gonzales whose love and kindness are without measure, plus Karen wrote one of the poems. Big thanks to my children, who love me and pray for me, and especially my daughter Eryn, who did so much for Judy and me, especially during my transplant in 2016. Last but not least, thank You, God; all glory and honor to you.

CONTENTS

About the Author

I was born in San Diego, California, to Joseph Charles Elliott and Lola Mae Anderson. My parents were divorced when I was just four or five years old, but my father always lived close to us. My mother remarried to Donald W. Phillips, who was in the Navy, and he eventually retired. My father remarried as well to Mary Taylor, who was a wonderful woman. I have an older sister ((Patricia Wilson) and brother (Daryl Sandaker); we have the same mother but different fathers. They never lived with me, but they did live in San Diego as well and I got to see them fairly often.

I graduated from Mission Bay High School in San Diego and then spent one year at Mesa Junior College in San Diego. I moved and went to live in Seattle, Washington, where I got married. I worked at Boeing, Plant 2, for one year. Since this was during the Vietnam War era, I got a draft notice but was able to join the U.S. Air Force just in time. I spent 20 years in the Air Force as a computer specialist and was stationed all over the U.S. and overseas. My favorite assignment was to RAF Greenham Common in Newberry, England. I actually lived in Streatley (Berkshire) during my four years there. I left England and my last assignment was to Onizuka AFB in Mt. View, California. After retirement I got my Bachelor's degree in Computer Information Systems from Chapman College. During my 22 years of marriage to my first wife, we had three children: Johnathan, Eryn, and David, but the marriage ended in divorce.

I was unemployed for a few months before I finally got a job with Lockheed Martin as a Satellite Systems Engineer. I eventually remarried Judy Elliott (the best thing I ever did), and we have been married for almost 31 years (Aug 14). I attended Western Seminary in San Jose, California, for two years with the intention of getting a Master's degree in Divinity. I have been teaching and preaching for over fifty years. Over the years, I have taught mainly Junior High and Senior High Sunday school classes, witnessing classes, adult Sunday school classes, and many adult bible studies. I also taught a bible study for five and a half years as a chaplain in Buckeye, Arizona. I have performed quite a few weddings and a few memorial services. I am still amazed at how and why God continues to use me – what a mighty God we serve.

Page Blank Intentionally

The Master Of The Storm

Though the wind surrounds me
And blows in my face
I cast my eyes toward Jesus
His glory and grace

The seas are mounting
They come crashing about,
But because of Jesus I do
Not fear or doubt.

Only when I lose my focus
On my Savior, on Him,
Do my feelings of drowning
And helplessness sinks in.

The Master of the Storm
The clouds and the seas
To worship my Lord Jesus
Is what I do please.

To trust in Him, the Lord
When He calls
Is the least I can do
For He gave me His all

-   Matt14:24-33

1

Let me tell you how that poem came about and the ones to follow. I had separated from my first wife of 20-plus years before we finally ended up in divorce. I was going through counseling at this point for about six months and was still an emotional mess. I was at work (Lockheed Martin/Satellite Systems Engineer), and I needed to go to the bathroom. While I was sitting down doing my thing this poem just came to me. I didn't ask God to give me a poem. I was good in English in high school and college, but I didn't write poems. These words just came to me in a matter of a few minutes; it was amazing. After I finished going to the bathroom I went straight back to my cubicle and wrote the words down that God had given me. It was an amazing feeling, and I really felt blessed and close to God. What I also didn't know is that God was not done with me yet, and there were a lot more poems to come, with most of them coming straight from God because I was listening to Him.

I think it is important for you to know my background a bit, which will help you understand me and my poems. I was born and raised in San Diego, California. I have a sister and a brother. We have the same mother but different fathers. They never lived with me but were in the San Diego area; I was the youngest and raised as an only child. It was pretty normal in the fact that my parents were alcoholics, and they smoked a lot. My Mom and Dad were divorced when I was only five or six years old (the third one for my mother), but my real father always lived quite close to us. My stepfather was in the Navy, and I didn't see him much because he was out to sea quite a bit. My parents loved me, and believe it or not, I never got spanked (I came close once); not that I was perfect, of course, but my Mom just didn't believe in doing that since I was basically raised by her. I never went to church as a kid because my mother was not a Christian or a religious person. In fact, she was a card-carrying member of the AAAA, which stands for American Association for the Advancement of Atheism, but she did love Christmas and Christmas music.

After graduating from High School (Mission Bay) and attending one year of Junior College, I moved to Seattle, got married, and started to work for Boeing (Plant 2). I was too young and not very mature. I was also an introvert (like the Apostle John) but came out of that to some degree over the years. My first wife was even younger but very mature for her age. She was a Type-A extravert (like the Apostles Peter and Paul). I managed to join the Air Force in 1968 before I got drafted, and my first duty assignment was in Massachusetts. We had our first child (son) in January of 1970, and in March of 1970, I got sent to Okinawa on a 4 ½ month temporary duty assignment in support of Viet Nam.

On May 1st of 1970 I gave my life to Jesus because some Army enlisted men came to my quarters and shared the gospel with me and told me that we are all sinners (Romans 3:23) and the wages of sin is death (Romans 6:23) but because of the sacrifice of Jesus on the cross and his blood that he shed we can have eternal life if we accept Him into our hearts (Revelation3:20). It is not by any works that we can do, money that we give to church or charities or trying to be good that gets us to heaven (Ephesians 3:8-9) but only by Jesus (John 14:6). By the time I left Okinawa I had read the New Testament, got started in a bible study and started the Topical Memory System and had memorized a number of bible verses. This was all because of an

3

organization called the Navigators, which still exists today.

Once I came back to Massachusetts, I got involved in teaching the High School kids at the Baptist church that we attended, and I continued teaching and preaching everywhere I went, thanks to the Air Force. From Massachusetts, I went to San Bernardino, California (where my other two children were born). Then I went to Stuttgart, Germany, for three years and from there to San Antonio, Texas, from there to Streatley, England, and lastly to San Jose, California. I retired in 1988, and my last assignment was at Onizuka AFB in Sunnyvale, California.

I would like to say that my marriage and family were wonderful and everything was fantastic but that would not be the truth. Over the years, my wife and I got further and further apart, and we were never really friends, especially best friends. My suggestion to anyone reading this who is married or getting married in the future is to make sure that your spouse is your best friend, and that you share everything with them and communicate freely and lovingly. Anyway, in 1990, my wife moved out of the house, and the kids were with me. I was an emotional wreck filled with anger, resentment, hatred, abandonment, loneliness, and more. We decided to get counseling from the senior pastor at the church we were attending. In the past, I had always said, "I don't need that." In reality I should have taken it because I did need it. After a while, my wife decided to drop out, but I decided to stay with it. My thought was I should be fine in six months of this counseling stuff, but I was very wrong. After 20 years of marriage and holding on to a lot of dysfunction in my life, I needed a lot more than six months of counseling. In fact, it took me over a year. One thing I must mention and this is **very important.** One night in the very beginning of when my wife left, I had a talk with God, and this is what I said, "OK God I have been with you and serving you for 20 years now, and look where I am, look where you put me, I have a decision to make and this is what I am thinking. I need to either give up on this Christianity stuff because it hasn't done me any good, or I should get just as close to you as I can possibly get and see what happens." Thankfully, I made the right decision, and that was to get as close to God as I could get. How do you do that? You read your Bible every day as much as you can. You talk to God just as if He is right next to you and be honest with Him. Another important thing that I learned was to **LISTEN** to God. We are so busy talking to Him that we don't take the time to listen. There were times when I could hear Him speak to me personally. There were times when someone I knew would tell me what God told them to tell me and times when I heard God through some ministers on the radio (Chuck Swindoll and Charles Stanley). One day, while driving, I was pounding on the steering wheel and screaming at God and blaming Him for my misery and emotional pain. You know what? He didn't strike me dead for yelling at Him; God understands where you are and knows what you are going through. He loves us so much and wants the very best for us (John 3:16). In the process of getting closer, it was amazing how he started to work on me and through me. I was very thankful for the counseling I was getting. I realized how dysfunctional I was and codependent. I had to deal with anger, abandonment that went back to my childhood, dealing with loneliness, and being alone; I also dealt with my kids, who were acting up because of the separation and, finally, the divorce. My first son, who was older (20) after staying at home for a while, moved out and was living with a friend. My daughter ended up in Juvenile Hall twice, and my younger son was at home with me, and I thought he was okay. I let him go to a church high school weekend retreat, and when I picked him up on Sunday, I asked him if he enjoyed himself and did he learn anything. He said, "Yes, I learned that I hate you." That made me feel great (not), but at least he was able to share his feelings.

As I had mentioned earlier I was an emotional mess in the beginning for the first twelve months especially. In the past, people would ask me how are you doing? My response would most likely be "fine or okay." I didn't know about true feelings except anger and pain. I saw a lot of that growing up; my Dad had a lot of anger, and my Mom had a lot of pain, emotional and physical. This next poem expresses my emotions and the pain that I was experiencing. This is actually the very first poem that I wrote about 4 months into my separation and counseling.

Emotions

The pain is agonizing it's more than I can bear

To feel so rejected, that no one really cares

You pour your heart out to be tramped in the dirt

The ones you love the most are the ones who cause the hurt.

There's darkness all around me and hope is not in sight

You wonder will this last forever, how can I make things right?

The tears that flow so often, frustration, anger and fear

The attacks come from all around me; I'm battered, worn and scared

Without my Lord Jesus life would not be worth living

As I read His word and hear His voice He keeps giving and giving.

There is hope; there is joy and peace within my soul

But days do come and Satan attacks and leaves a great big hole.

Oh Lord my God only you can fix the hurt, the pain, the feelings

Of despair

I know, really know how much you love and care.

There will be times when you are going through difficulties in your life that you feel like "Nobody cares." It isn't true, but you sure feel that way. You feel anger, pain, loneliness, and maybe even resentment, but the one thing that I learned early in my recovery is that God always cares, and He wants to make you whole. Even though He had twelve apostles, He knew from the beginning that one of them would betray Him but he still loved him the same as the others and cared for each and every one. He cared enough to heal the blind (John 9), cleanse the leper and heal the deaf (Matthew 11:5), and raise the dead (John 11).

He Cares

Only God can heal the pain of loneliness
Come close to Him and His caress.
His love for you which knows no bounds
Will fill your heart and wipe away the frowns.
Oh come close to Him my child, and seek His face
Because no one can match His care and grace.
He wants to spend special time with you alone
So get away from the television and the phone.
He cares, really cares for us can't you see
Because He gave His Son to die for us on that tree
No pain that you have, no problem that you see
Are too big for our Lord Jesus, the man from Galilee

My next poem came about due to the fact that when you grow closer to God the positive thing is that you can really feel His presence and hear Him talking to you. One time, I was attending a three-day seminar on dealing with your inner child which was very beneficial. Most of our issues and dysfunction come from our early childhood. I already knew this, but it was reinforced when I took some counseling courses in Seminary in 1995. Anyway, there was one time when I rescued my inner child from a home we lived in when I was only eight years old. I took him out of the house and was told to go to a safe place. As I rounded the corner, there was Jesus standing there with His arms wide open, and we both ran to Him and got such a wonderful hug, and He told me everything will be fine. What a wonderful experience

The negative thing about getting close to God is that you can expect the devil to attack you because he doesn't want you to get close to God and be an effective Christian, telling others about the good news of the gospel and about Jesus. The one story that I am reminded of when it comes to being attacked by Satan is when I was asked to give my testimony at a Men's weekend retreat. I knew it was going to be good because every time I rehearsed it, I would cry like a baby. I told God that my goal was to please and glorify the Lord in my talk. I even asked a friend of mine to stay close when I start to talk in case I get so emotional I would need him to be next to me and help me get through it. My thinking was, I just know Satan is going to try and attack me somehow. Well, I was right. Even before I left the house to go to church, I went to my son's room, and in plain sight were two or three Playboy magazines. I asked my son where he got those, and he said that he got them from a friend. I told him he could not have them (he was too young) and that I would have to dispose of them. As I grabbed them, the temptation was strong. My brain said, *"It's okay if you look at them, you are old enough, it's not a big deal."* That voice was not God or from God so I held strong in the Lord and did not look (James 4:7-8a). I was going to throw them in the trash in the garage, but I thought my son just might go looking for them while I was away, so I hid them and threw them away when I got back.

My testimony was even better than I had hoped. I was able to get through it even if I cried like a baby, and when I looked at the 125 men in the audience, they were all crying as well. The main speaker came after me and said that it was a fantastic testimony. I thought Satan tried to defeat me, but with God on your side, you have the victory. There are two verses in **Romans chapter 8** that are very helpful to believers in Christ:

28 And we know that God causes all things to work together for good to those who love God, to those who are called according to His purpose...

31 what then shall we say to these things? If God is for us, who is against us?

On the way home from the retreat, I was thinking again, *"You know Satan was defeated at the retreat I wonder if he will try something else when I get back to try and defeat me?"* We got back to the church, and my minivan was supposed to be there, but it was missing. I sure hope it wasn't stolen so a friend gave me a lift back to my house which was close. When I got home, my minivan was not there either. I came into the house, and my son and daughter were both sitting in the front room, looking suspicious and fearful.

I said, "Where is the minivan?"

My daughter spoke up and said sheepishly, "I took it, Dad, and it broke on the way back."

In the past, I would start yelling and screaming and cursing, but this time I was ready. You know what I did? I started to laugh, and I laughed for quite a while as my children looked at me like I was crazy. I told them about the retreat and how I knew Satan was going to try and defeat me, but I was strong in the Lord and had just come down from the Mountain top like Moses. Long story short, my minivan's clutch was ruined and my daughter had to pay for it since she stole the car without permission.

The Enemy Surrounds Me

The enemy surrounds me and wants to cast me down
What do I do, do I worry, fret or frown?
No, I cast my eyes toward heaven and I give a great big shout

Thank God, Praise Jesus! I will not fear or doubt.
I look in the eye of the devil and I tell him outright,
I've been covered by the blood of Jesus; He is my guide and light.

I've been beaten and bruised and lost everything
But Jesus my Lord, my Savior and King
Picks up the pieces and heals everything.
When fear grips me in the eye of the storm
Do I get down and depressed and look forlorn?

No, I surface in the strength of Jesus and look in His face
I'm strong and courageous and grow in the faith.
My God is in control, He's majestic and serene
He's awesome and beautiful, greater than anything.

This next poem came while I was still in counseling, and as I had said before, it took a lot longer than I thought it would take to get emotionally healthy, but well worth the effort. I have witnessed many people who are dysfunctional in one form or another, and they end up in divorce. They don't bother to get any help with their issues and remarry within a few months. The dysfunction that you had doesn't go away, and you end up carrying it with you (like a backpack) wherever you go. Before you know it you end up in divorce again. If you are dysfunctional, your children will be as well, and the cycle continues until you get some help from a professional counselor, preferably a Christian counselor. People will tell you, even counselors, that you should not make any decisions based on your feelings. Don't go grocery shopping when you feel hungry. Don't buy a new car when you are upset with your spouse. Don't go home and yell and scream at the family because you got laid off from work. But you can take those negative feelings and turn them into positive ones. Take your anger and turn it into love and joy. It's your decision. Ask God to take away the anguish that you feel and turn it into peace. Take away the loneliness and turn it into being alone with God.

Feelings

God has given us feelings of loneliness and pain
But they're not for hurt, they are designed for gain.
Don't run and hide, don't give in
Come close to the one who made you, come close to Him.
When you feel depressed, exhausted and mad
Tell it all to Jesus, he cares that you feel sad.
Have you been abandoned, have you lost a loved one or friend?
His arms are wide open for you to come in.
If you want to know the joy of God, don't feel afraid to cry
He alone can heal you He will wipe your tears dry.
When Moses said to love the Lord with all of your might
He meant to love Him with your feelings and not your sight.

There is one line in that poem that says, *"Have you been abandoned, have you lost a loved one or friend?"* During this time frame and shortly before I wrote this poem, my mother passed away. She was everything to me; she was the one that raised me. Even though my real father lived close by, he didn't raise me, and my stepfather was in the Navy and gone a lot. Even when he was home, he and I were never close. My mother died of cancer of the throat because she was a heavy smoker. When I was 17, I went to the doctor with her, and he told her that the cancer she had was from smoking and she should stop. She did stop for a while but not for very long, and the cancer came back, and she passed away when she was 75.

This next poem was actually one of the last poems I wrote but I thought it should go here since I was just talking about my mother and how much she loved me and cared for me. I think of her and my father often.

Mom and Her Love

My mother never talked about God in a positive way

Her father yelled, screamed and made her obey.

My mother never told me of God and His plan

She was told she couldn't do anything not even please a man.

My mother never experienced love the way it should be, but with all her shortcomings I knew she loved me.

All the things that she missed, all the loving and care

She gave to her little boy, the one she thought so fair.

My mother never told me of God up above

But I know I know God because of her love.

Another thing you should know is that when you give your life wholeheartedly to God your life might turn out like Job. First, Satan approached God the Father and wanted to take everything away from Job, which God granted. He lost everything, family, and possessions; in fact, *his wife even told him, "Do you still hold firm your integrity? Curse God and die!"* (Job 2:9) Then his three friends came, and instead of encouraging Job told him how wrong he was and how sinful he must be. But Job fell to the ground and worshiped God. *He said, "Naked I came from my mother's womb, and naked I shall return there. The LORD gave and the LORD has taken away. Blessed be the name of the LORD."* (Job 1:21)

During my time in counseling and going through my divorce, I lost some friends, but I gained some as well. I also had some people give me advice that was not from God because the Holy Spirit in me told me that what they were saying was not biblical or from the Lord. As I mentioned earlier that is the importance of listening to God. I went through my journals recently, and what I noticed were two main things: **(1)** God was always there for me and gave me exactly what I **needed** (not wanted) when I needed it, even if it was a reprimand or He made me wait instead of providing me what I thought I needed immediately. **(2)** I was amazed at how many Christian friends, even one that wasn't a Christian, spent time with me, encouraging me and praying either with me or for me. If you are going through a difficult time, either with depression, a lost loved one, medical problems, stress, or whatever, you need prayer from others. I am asked all the time to pray for someone or something, and I love doing it.

I am writing these poems in pretty much chronological order, so this next one has to do with prayer which is crucial to the Christian life. Think about it: your close friends and your best friend are people that you spend more time with, talking and listening to. So, if you want to get close to the Lord, then spend more time with Him, talking and listening.

Prayer

Prayer, what a wonderful gift from the Lord on high
To reach up and talk to our heavenly Father in the sky
He wants to hear our troubles, sorrows and joys
He wants to hear from all his precious girls and boys
He loves when you come close and you whisper to Him
"Oh Lord can you help me, I really need a friend."
When tears of pain come streaming down your face
He hears every whimper and gives you His strength and grace
Honor, glory and praise, we need to bring
To our heavenly Father, Lord and King
Come to Him in humbleness, not demanding to be heard
Seek Him in gentleness and in His holy word

Pray for all others; hold them up in His sight
Pray for their protection, love, guidance and might
Some may say to pray is the least you can do
But that's not true; it is the most you can do
So get on your knees, pray for love joy and peace
Pray for your friends, give praise to the Three, never cease.

Back to my counseling time and difficulties in my life, I didn't realize how dysfunctional I was until I started counseling. This reminds me of when I went to get a massage. I didn't think my back was that sore or messed up, but when the masseuse started all of a sudden, she found all kinds of knots in my back, and she said, "You have a lot of stress." I told a friend of mine one day while we had our walk and prayer time that people are like a pretty little lake; on the surface, it's nice and glassy, smooth and calm, but just a little way underneath the surface, there is a lot of mud, rocks, and gunk. We are like that to some people; we look nice and calm and serene, but underneath, there is a lot of emotional clutter that needs to be cleaned up. It is great to know that God wants the best for you and He really cares about you and loves you dearly, hence this next poem.

Hang On

Thru the fire of life we continue on

Thru the winds of time life goes from dawn to dawn

When it seems like you can't keep going

When the storms keep thundering and the winds keeps blowing

Just remember our Lord fought the fight

To keep you justified and secure in His sight

If your focus strays from the one on high

You will stumble, fall on your face and cry

His love for you has no bounds

He will take away the pain and wipe away the frowns.

At times it seems that life isn't fair

But believe me my precious God really cares

He is faithful, loving, wonderful and true

He has your best in mind and will make you brand new

How do I know because He has the best view?

At this point I am starting to do a lot better with my life; I have been in counselling for over a year and not going that often compared to going once a week in the beginning, now it's just once a month. Not only am I becoming more functional but less angry, codependent, lonely, and feelings of abandonment. Putting these counselling words out reminds me of the list of positive aspects that the bible talks about concerning Love in **1 Corinthians 13:4-8a.**

⁴ Love is patient, love is kind, it is not jealous; love does not brag, it is not arrogant. ⁵ It does not act disgracefully, it does not seek its own benefit; it is not provoked, does not keep an account of a wrong suffered, ⁶ it does not rejoice in unrighteousness, but rejoices with the truth; ⁷ it [b]keeps every confidence, it believes all things, hopes all things, endures all things.⁸ Love never fails;

Stepping back about a year, the reason I put Corinthians here is that there was a one-time frame when I had only been in counseling for six months or less when God convicted me of these verses. I had two main goals when I started counseling: the first one was to salvage my marriage, and the second goal was to become emotionally and mentally healthy. When I read these verses, I realized that I was not doing any of them. I was not patient, I was not kind, I was jealous, I was arrogant, and I did act in a disgraceful manner so forth and so on. Then I started to cry (I did that a lot for an entire year). There was one time when I was at work running a satellite support. I was at the time a Ground Controller we also had a Mission Controller and a Planner Analyst. One of my jobs was to take screen prints at certain times during the support. My mind was not on my job but on my pending divorce and all the emotions I was going through. When the Mission

Controller asked me if I had done the screen prints all I could do was look at him and start to cry. My Mission Controller understood and so did God. Moving forward to where I ended the previous page (counselling for over a year) this next poem is one that I felt in my heart and God helped me to write this one as well. I just felt so thankful for everything that God had done and what He was doing in my life.

I love the **book of Psalms** but one of my favorites is **9:1-2**

[1]I will praise You, O LORD, with my whole heart;

I will tell of all Your marvelous works.

[2]I will be glad and rejoice in You

I will sing praise to Your name, O Most High.

Poem To The Lord

I want to write a poem Lord to tell you how wonderful you are
How your glory shines in the heavens brighter than any star.
As each and every day goes by, I'm beginning to understand
That you are making me more and more into a Christ like man
The pain that I've suffered the sorrow and fear
Are strengthening my soul and helping me to see clear
How much you really love me, how much you truly care
You're always there when I need you, like a breath of fresh air.
Praise and worship are words that I know
But there are so many times when actions I don't show.
I try so very hard to put you at first
And I hunger for your word and your prayers I do thirst.
Please forgive me dear Father for my selfish attitude
For the way that I'm unloving, uncaring and rude
I'm so thankful for Jesus who died
Who rose into heaven and sits at your side
He has rescued my little boy and counts every tear
He whispers right to me, "I love you my child, you have nothing to fear."
Jesus, the first and the last, good shepherd and friend
You've guided me from beginning and you'll be there at the end.
I thank you dear Father for sending to me
Some wonderful, loving people who prayed on their knees,
To uphold me, encourage, strengthen and show
That the Lord really loves me and wants me to grow
Father in closing I just want to say
I look forward to loving you, and knowing you more each and every day.

When you are going through a difficult time in your life, and everything just seems to keep piling up, and you think it can't get any worse, guess what? It gets worse. I remember one time I was by myself in front of my pastor, who was counseling me, and he said, "Things are never as bad as you think they are, and they are never as good as you think they are." I left his office and thought that didn't help me any, but down the road, I thought those were really important words that I needed at the time. I also remember when I was going through all of my stuff: a marriage that was failing (it had been for years), dealing with anger, abandonment, loneliness, and codependency, to name a few, and then there were the children. One got kicked out of school and had to go to a school for misbehaved kids. Another one almost got kicked out of school because they decided that they didn't need to do any homework, and the third one was also an emotional mess for a while. I prayed to God and said, "Lord, it can't get any worse and I am thankful that I at least have good health." The next day, my back went out, and I was in a lot of pain for a while; I should have prayed, Lord, thank you that I don't have a million dollars and live in Hawaii. Anyway, this next poem came about actually as I was reading my Bible. I came across a couple of verses in Psalm 20, and the next thing you know, God gave me this poem. We need to feel safe and secure when we are dealing with difficulties in our lives. Just remember God has you and won't let go (I will never leave you or forsake you) **Hebrews 13:5.**

Safe And Secure

He tenderly nudges and tells us to go.

He wants nothing but the best for us,

To make us like Him

To humble our hearts and cleanse us from sin

When we follow Him closely and we listen with care

He melts us and molds us and He's always right there.

Step by step and day by day

That is what He wishes, and He wants us to pray.

Our strength comes from our God of course

Not from a chariot or from a horse.

Father, Son, Holy One, all one and the same,

We praise you Lord of host, we praise your Holy name.

-   Psalm 20

At this point in my life I was done with my counselling and God was working on some amazing things, two things especially. The first one was that I had an amazing outreach at work. Since I was sharing with everyone all the things that I was going through and how God was with me all the time, and started to share some of my poems with them. In fact, a couple of the people at work who were Christians told me, "You should write a book, your poems are amazing." It only took me 30 years later to finally decide to do just that. The second thing that God gave me is a female friend. When I first got divorced, I said, "I am never getting married again." After a year or so, I said, "If I do get married, this is what I am looking for: someone who puts God first in their life, someone who respects me, someone that I can talk to and pray with them, someone that loves me just the way I am, that doesn't want to change me." I didn't ask for a beautiful woman on the outside but a beautiful woman on the inside. I was looking for a Proverbs 31 woman, and that is exactly what God gave me plus, He even gave me a beautiful woman on the outside as well.

Let me tell you about our first date. Actually, I can't remember because neither of us knew when we had a first date. We started off as acquaintances; we went to the same church and belonged to the same ministry (Operation Love). This ministry was an outreach ministry that was geared toward sharing with people who lived in the local area about our church (large) and all the programs that they had for all ages. If people had questions about God/Jesus, we were all trained to share the gospel.

Anyway, at first, I would just invite Judy to some work activities that we were having, for instance, a beach day with volleyball and food.

One time, we all went to a Halloween outdoor carnival. We spent a lot of time together especially praying and talking together. I will tell you more later, but for now, I just want to share the next poem that God gave me dealing with finally getting better emotionally and spiritually. I thought this day would never come because it took so long, but God's timing is not our timing.

Love And Follow

Oh Lord is there anything about you that hasn't been said before

You're the one I worship, love and adore.

You have begun a good work in me, you promised from the start

You promised you would always be there, and not leave me

In the dark

A God like you who's strong and true, a trusted friend indeed

Your love surrounds and abounds and there's nothing else I need.

The joy inside makes me laugh and smile and peace calms my

Very soul

Once I was blind but now I can see, you have healed me and made

Me whole

Oh lord I really love you and I wish you were here with me

I'd give you a great big hug, and kiss you tenderly.

I'm not sure what you've got planned for me, I really do not know

But I look forward to each new day with you, and where you lead I

will go.

I really like the second to last line, *"I'm not sure what you've got planned for me."* Because it was so amazing what God had planned for me, when you get close to God and put Him first in everything, He will definitely use you. I can't tell you how He will use you or where because everyone is different, just like it says in scripture; some of us are legs, some are arms, some are mouths and some are eyes, but we all fit together in God's family (**Romans 12:3-8; 1Corinthians 12**).

This next poem just came to me a month and a half after the last one. Judy and I had gone to Monterey so I could run a 10k race. We had a great time for the day there, enjoying the beautiful surroundings and watching people doing hand gliding, and I had a good time with my run. It was wonderful being able to have fun and enjoy life again, especially with someone who appreciates and loves you.

Love And Grace

I don't deserve the love and grace

That He so freely shines upon my face.

The joy and peace that fills my soul

Has turned an ugly life into one that is beautiful and whole

My spirit soars above and beyond

To reach up and touch the Holy, awesome One

To be near Him in His presence is grand

And I love how He guides me in the palm of His hand.

As I gaze into the wondrous night

I behold His majesty and might.

When I look at the hills, trees, valleys and rivers

I am amazed, awe inspired and my heart starts to quiver.

I praise you my God with my heart, soul and might

I praise you my Lord in the morning, noon and night.

I had mentioned earlier that Judy was now in my life, and the more time we spent together, the more I really enjoyed her company. Even though she was divorced and her two sons lived in the area, she did not have a home to live in but was renting a room in one house when I first met her. That did not work out because the husband that lived there was hitting on her, so she moved to another home where it was her and another lady. At times, she would call me over to help her with moving things or fixing her car and I was glad that I was able to help her out. One day, I invited her to go rafting, but this time, it was an overnight trip, and we were going to have to share a tent. One thing that we both agreed on was that even before we decided to get married, we pledged that we would not have pre-marital sex, and that is exactly what we did. I must admit that it was difficult at times for me. I am a Christian, but I was a man first, and we have our hormones to deal with, but God is so faithful and knew that we both had put Him first and not the flesh.

Watch and pray, lest you enter into temptation. The spirit indeed *is* willing, but the flesh *is* weak."

- *Matthew 26:41*

We had a great time on our rafting trip with my Lockheed buddies. We drove all the way to Ashland, Oregon, to go down the Upper Klamath River, which was a class 4 experience. It was an amazing trip and a ton of fun, but boy, did we get wet. Our guide was great and very professional. Afterward, God gave me this next poem, which I really love; not only did it explain our trip but how life is at times.

The Rapids Of Love

When life seems like a roaring rapids trip

And you get tossed and turned and start to flip.

Hang on tight to the raft of God

Keep your eyes ahead, don't be afraid and paddle on.

With the water in your face, you need His gift of grace

Down you go, oh so low you can't seem to keep pace.

Gasping for air, sometimes life doesn't seem fair

But you hold onto the oar of the word and you go forward

In His care

After a few that you've gone thru, you come to a resting place,

You gather your strength through prayer, and prepare to

Continue the race.

Later on when you start to have fun you realize it wasn't just you

There are others in the boat that helped you get through

And your guide, who was always at your side to help you feel like new

When you hit the next rapid your confidence soars,

Because you know in the boat the Lord holds the oars.
You're wrapped in the Spirit with your life jacket of love,

It fits very snugly, because it comes from the Father above.

Your wetsuit of truth keeps you so dry,

But God says it's O.K. if you really need to cry.

The helmet of salvation will protect you from harm,

If you listen closely to your guide there is no need for alarm.

Safe and secure our guide is the best,

He'll steer you past the dangers and lead you to rest.

He's been where you are and He's gone twice as far.

So trust in your guide, there's no need to hide.

You made it thru, just like His promises to you are true.

It was now the beginning of 1993, and things were getting serious with Judy and me. This next poem is not about the Lord, but it is how the Lord gives you what you pray for and Judy was definitely an answer to prayer. I mentioned earlier that it is important that your mate needs to be your best friend, and that is what Judy is to me. From an acquaintance, to a friend, to a best friend, to a wife that's the proper Godly steps for marriage.

My Best Friend

In my time of desperation, God did send

A beautiful, wonderful and loving best friend

You've taught me so much of God's perfect plan

You helped me to see and be all that I can.

I couldn't have made it without your tender care

In my tears and my sorrows you were always right there.

When I have trouble understanding God's love and grace

I study your eyes, your smile and see God's love in your face.

Your calm and gentile spirit settles me down,

I feel so at ease when you are around.

I love to be near you, to hold you so tight,

To take care of you when you're hurting just seems so right.

There isn't anything I wouldn't do for you, can't you see?

I know you understand, because you'd do it for me.

When you tell me that you pray and give me

Over to God each and every day my heart feels so humble,

Inspired and proud I could soar like an eagle

In the highest of clouds

You are so special, so beautiful and precious my love

I'm so thankful to God that He sent me His perfect dove.

This next poem is not mine, but it just goes to show you what I said earlier: that I wanted a Godly woman in my life, one that puts God first, and that is exactly what Judy was and is to this day. I guess I inspired her to write a poem since she had read all of mine, so this next one is from Judy to me.

Free Bird

Free bird fly home to Thee

Sing your song of praise with glee

Love has healed you and is making you whole

Able now to fulfill your role

So fly high in the clouds just as high as you can

For you are now God's beautiful man

Most of my poems had a date when I wrote them, but there were a couple that had no date, so I just put them in where I thought they best fit. This next one falls into that category. I could have left it out altogether, but I really like it, and I think you will as well.

Hello God

Hello God, how are you today?
I just want you to know that I'm doing OK.
I really want to thank you for getting me through
A very tough time that only a few make it through.
You shaped and molded someone I admire,
You've taken my anger and put out that fire.
You've replaced the turmoil with love, peace and joy
You retrieved and you loved my lost little boy.
By putting you first in all that I do
You have given me strength to be just like you.
I have so much fun being just who I am
I don't have to pretend, I owe all to the Lamb.
My witness is natural, it's nice being free
Now they really hear Jesus and not little old me.
At first when the tribulation and trials came along
I couldn't believe what I did was so wrong.
But you loved me and showed me and helped me to see
That I was in the care of Jesus, I was a limb on the tree.
Now I can praise you because I know what you've done
You took someone ugly, who was prideful and glum,
And turned him into something beautiful, who truly loves
The three in one

I don't remember the date exactly but I do remember the day. It was a Saturday, and I had come to the conclusion that I wanted Judy to be my wife, and I was ready to propose to her. I had the evening all planned out; I was going to take her out to a really nice steak restaurant in downtown San Jose, and after we ate, I would take her to see the play "Annie." I had already purchased the tickets for the play. I wrote a little poem and was going to read it at the restaurant and give her the ring that I had purchased. The only problem was that the restaurant was quite dark and I couldn't see my poem so I had to wait until we were finished and go to the car and read it to her there. "I'm sorry to say that I don't have the poem for you to see, but she did say "Yes," and we had a great night."

I am now going to tell you about the most wonderful pre-wedding and wedding miracles, along with a couple of poems. We both believed that before we got married, we must have pre-marital counseling. Not only did we take one but three different courses. Two were just a long weekend, but the other one was two weeks long. We had set a date of August 14th, and we were ready to send out wedding invitations. At the last minute, the pastor said we could not get married at his church because he didn't think I was ready. This was the same pastor who had counseled me for over a year, but I hadn't seen him in nearly two years because we were going to a different church. We were already set to get married on that date, so now what do we do? We prayed, of course, so Judy and I prayed; first, was I ready or not? We wanted to hear it from God, and second was the date available at the church we were attending? We both felt that God was telling us that we were both emotionally, spiritually, and physically ready to get married.

Now, what about the date? We went to the church (quite large) to see if we could get the date we wanted. They told us that summertime is the time everyone wants to get married, and they were booked; the only date they had open was August 14th; what an answer to prayer.

Judy and I both agreed that we did not want to spend a lot of money on our wedding but we did want a nice honeymoon. One thing that Judy insisted on was she said, "I don't want to spend more than $100 on a wedding dress." As you all know, that is impossible to find a wedding dress at that price, but Judy and I prayed about it and we waited to see how God was going to provide. Speaking of providing, God did just that for everything. I had a lady friend at my work; she was an orbit analyst, but she also made wedding cakes on the side; she said she would do our wedding cake for free as a wedding present (it was fabulous). I had another friend at work that did videos at weddings and he said he would do ours for free. Another work buddy played the organ and he did our music. Another friend of ours from church was a great singer, so she sang some songs for the wedding. Another close friend of mine from work had an old classic car (1948 Nash Ambassador), so he drove us from the house to the church and back in a cool old car. We decided to have the reception at my house, so about five ladies from my work came over to the house, decorated it, and helped cook the food that we got, mostly from Costco.

I bet you are wondering about the wedding dress and did God provided. So, one day, Judy left her place where she was staying and had to go to the grocery store to pick up a few things. There was no parking available in front of the store, so she ended up parking not too far away in front of Goodwill. As she got out of the car, she looked at the store window, and in the window, there was a sign that read "Jessica McClintock" wedding dresses for $99, and there were quite a few to choose from. Needless to say she was over the top and amazed at how God provided. This next poem is one that I wrote about a week before the wedding.

The Happiest Man In The World

Oh Lord, Dear Lord you have made me the happiest man in the world
You have given me the most wonderful, precious, beautiful girl
And gave her all your goodness, fruitfulness and light
Your ways are not my ways it is so very clear, and your thoughts
Are not mine but what I do know is you are always so near
The tears that I shed, those years gone by did not go to waste or
Just evaporate in the sky.
My heart reached out to you and we got so very close, you knew me
Better than anyone and you knew what I needed most
I wasn't looking for love, a relationship or spouse
In fact most of the time I just wanted to be left alone in the house
But you had other plans of your own it is plain to see
You wanted to give your child Judy to little old me
She has been my very best friend a man could ever have
A joy and a treasure, she is most excellent bodacious and fab
All kidding aside Dear Father I feel so humble and unworthy
My heart skips a beat when I walk down the street and I
Think of how lucky I am
To be getting married to someone so wonderful, beautiful and
Precious, just like your sacrificial lamb
Oh Yes dear Lord I sing and I shout to you in the sky
Because to me you have given an angel from on high
I pray dear Lord that you will bless us with many years together
Because I want to love her always, and let go of her – never

It was now the day of the wedding, and everything was perfect. I remember that the pastor said to us, "It is normal for the bride to be late, so don't worry if one or both of you are late." We were there on time and guess who was late – the pastor. We handed out the ceremony details to all attending, which was on one side, but on the other side was a poem that I had written for the wedding

Down the isle of matrimony

Her beauty radiates the room

As she steps up to the alter

To join her loving groom

Both focused on the Lord Jesus Christ

As they promise to love and obey

In sickness and in health to serve

Each other day after dayRings on their fingers

As both say I will

Two hearts beating together

God has joined them both

In His perfect will

So let us rejoice and be glad

For we have witnessed today

Two loving and caring individuals

Together forever this very day

The wedding was fantastic and so was the reception. We decided that instead of spending the night at our house we would get a hotel close to the San Francisco Airport since we were leaving the next day for Honolulu, Hawaii. Our wedding was on a Saturday, so our flight was on Sunday. As we got to the airport and checked in I noticed that there was a local TV camera crew there interviewing people. Not only that, but what they were saying was there was a hurricane that was heading toward Honolulu and were people afraid to travel? I told Judy I wanted to get interviewed so I walked over to the lady doing the interviews. She asked me where we were going and I told her Honolulu, Hawaii. She asked me if I was afraid concerning our flight, and this is what I said, "We just got married yesterday, and it was a Godly wedding. I know that God will take care of that hurricane for us, and I am not afraid." Well, I just knew that my interview was not going to be aired because I was talking about God, but that was okay. About halfway to Hawaii, the captain of the plane came on the loudspeaker to say, "Folks, don't worry. It seems that the hurricane has moved out of our way, and we are safe to land as planned." God the provider, as mentioned earlier, our entire wedding was God-centered, and He got the glory. It gives me goosebumps just to write this down again to remember how wonderful God is.

When we came back from Hawaii and I had to go back to work because of the security clearance I possessed I had to go through a gate and then show a guard my badge. When I did that, the guard said, "I saw you on TV talking about your wedding and trip to Hawaii and how you had no fear."

Just a little over two months after our wedding (the first year we celebrated every month), I wrote another poem. This particular poem wasn't about the present but more about the past.

Rain, Wind, Sleet And Hail

Rain, wind, sleet, and hail, coming from all sides,
There's nowhere to go and nowhere to hide.
It engulfs me and takes control of my being
No matter what I do I'm haunted by this feeling.
Will it never end, how long can I go?
God promised sunshine, and to turn my winter to spring,
But the flowers are all dead and the birds never sing.
As I go a little further the weather isn't quite as bad
There is a glimpse of some daylight and I don't feel
Quite so sad
My steps still seem heavy, and my face has no smile,
But as I keep my focus straight ahead I know I can go one
More mile
Through the muddy trenches, through the forest so thick
I get scratched, banged and bruised, but never do I quit.
What I thought was going to be just a little hike
Has turned into an everlasting journey that I really do not like
On a little further the stormy trip starts to clear up.
The sleet and hail have gone; the wind and rain have nearly
subsided,
Once I thought I was all alone I now know that I have been guided
The further I go the more courageous and stronger I become
The feelings of loneliness, abandonment, anger and glum
Are all but gone, and I don't feel so inferior and dumb.

Yes, even along the trail there has been death, sorrow and despair
But the closer I get to the finish, the fresher the air.
I'm almost out of the forest and on the other side,
I know I couldn't have made it without my trusted guide.

Six months have gone by, and we are still so very much in love. When I say we, I mean Judy, God, and me. I am still very happy at work at this point I am now a Mission Controller. I think it's' pretty cool that I get to command a satellite circling the earth. My ministry at work is still doing great, but I feel like I should be doing more. My prayer life has changed over the years; in the beginning, I had very little time for God and it was almost all about me or my family. As time progressed, my prayer life changed from me to the Lord and more time to <u>listen to God</u>. Jesus, with his busy schedule and with people around Him all the time, had to get away to a secluded place to talk to the Father. Some people say you need to read your Bible and pray first thing in the morning, and that is fine for most people. But what about those of us who work a swing shift (4 to midnight) or work a grave shift (midnight to 8)? I actually read my Bible most of the time at night, around 9:30 or 10:00, because I am almost always up to midnight or later, and I pray all day long. This next poem is dedicated to prayer. I believe it is the most important thing we can do as Christians. What an awesome opportunity to be able to talk to God at any time, any place and about anything. People ask me to pray for their dog or cat. Do I tell them God doesn't care about your pet – No, He cares about us and what is important to us.

Pray

There is nothing on earth comparable to prayer

To speak to the Mighty Creator who really and truly cares.

You're not just wasting words when you give a holler

You don't have to give Him anything, not even a dollar.

He just wants of your time, to let Him know how you feel

He definitely is concerned about you, because He is for real.

If your heart is heavy laden with worries or fret

If you are worried about your loved ones or heavy in debt,

Don't be discouraged, don't give up and pout,

God, your heavenly Father is always there, don't ever doubt.

He counts every tear that rolls down your face

Not a one will be discarded they are easy to trace.

He knows your every need, before you even pray

But He loves to hear and listen and help you along the way.

So praise to the Father, the Spirit and Son

Pray for repentance, to be close to the One.

Pray for all others, there is nothing better you can do

And last but not least, you can speak to the Lord about you.

Here is an acrostic to help you to pray

P   *Praise the Lord first (Our Father who art in heaven, hallowed be thy name Matthew 6:9-10)*

R   *Repentance (if we confess our sins He is faithful and just to forgive us of our sins (1Johm 1:9)*

A   *All others   (Colossians 1:3)*

Y   *Yourself   (Matthew 26:36-44)*

It was 1995, and I have been married for two whole years. My strength and confidence in God is still very strong. I am active at church teaching, and again, my ministry at work is going very well. God says in His word to be a witness for Him which is difficult for an introvert like me.

But you shall receive power when the Holy Spirit has come upon you; and you shall be witnesses to Me in Jerusalem, and in all Judea and Samaria, and to the end of the earth."

-    *Acts 1:8*

But there are many ways to witness to someone. They can see how you act at work or play. Are you a witness with your mouth or your actions? Yes, we all are an ambassador for Christ. I have been trained in three different types of witnessing programs. The first one was the Navigators bridge illustration; the second one was Campus Crusade for Christ's Four Spiritual Laws; and the third one was Dr. James Kennedy's Evangelism Explosion, which I also taught for two years.

After Judy and I spent time in prayer about this next portion of my life, we decided that I should go to the Seminary. My thinking was *I will get a Masters in Divinity (M.Div.), quit my job as a Satellite engineer, and then become a senior pastor somewhere.* I was accepted at Western Seminary. The main campus was in Portland, Oregon but they had a satellite campus in San Jose. It was expensive, but I was using my VA money from the military. You had two options with the M.Div. You could either get the degree with a theological emphasis or a counseling emphasis. I have been doing a lot of counseling over the years, so I decided to get the degree with a counseling emphasis. I started in August of 95, and my first two courses were New Testament 1 and 2.

Shortly after I started seminary, I wrote another poem; I think I might have been inspired by Arnold Schwarzenegger (True Lies), as you will see.

Comfort

Lord where can I go when things don't seem right?

There is no comfort in a bottle or a can,

There is no lasting comfort from a woman or a man.

There is no real comfort in the Great Outdoors,

There is no comfort at the malls or the stores.

I can't stay busy enough or sit in a pew

To get real comfort Lord, what do I do?

Should I read a long novel that will make me forget?

How about a movie with Arnie flying a jet?

Maybe a challenging game of Parcheesi or chess

Turn on the TV and flip through the mess.

No, these don't really help me they just get in the way

The comfort they provide just doesn't stay.

Only you Lord can give the comfort I need

According to your word (II Cor. 1) it is abundant in time of need

When things are despairing and the world seems a mess,

When work is long and tasking and I never seem go get

Enough rest.

The children are so needing, should I help or not

At times I feel the world is so big and I'm just a little dot.

Yet, in all of this you are the rock of my salvation

I know I can come to you for peace and relaxation.

Your yoke is easy and you've asked me to take it

(Matt 11:28-30)

To find rest for my soul and to learn to be whole

This is my comfort in my affliction

That thy word has revived me, there can be no

Other addiction

Praise you Lord for what you have done

Praise you Lord for all that you do

Praise you Lord for helping me through

Praise you Lord - There is no one like You

I must admit I really enjoyed seminary but it was hard on me. I remember there was only one course that I had to drop and that was Hebrew, not the book of Hebrews but the language Hebrew. The main thing was working all the hours I had to work, and going to school was, at times, too much. I was taking at least two courses per semester; once, I took three.

It was June or July of 96 that I wrote this next poem, and it had to do with my dad. I really miss him; he was such a great guy. He had his problems when I was younger, but when he married my stepmother, he really got his life straight, and just before he passed away, he accepted Jesus into his life. I learned how to treat people from my dad; he treated everyone with respect, compassion, and love. I saw him give the shirt off his back to someone who needed it more than him. I saw him lend his truck to someone who needed it more than he did that day. It didn't matter if you were male or female, if you were red, white, or black, and he really loved me. He died of Hodgkin's cancer way too young. He was only 57 years old.

Father's Day

Father's Day is upon us and it is time to reminisce

Why didn't my father hug me, why didn't he give me a kiss?

All the promises that were broken, all the times that he said

I'm sorry my dear boy, I was home drunk in bed.

I really wanted to know him, to get close inside

But he stayed so far from me; I lay on my bed and cried.

On many occasions I saw him rant and rave

His anger uncontrollable, like a storm curling wave

Even though he never told me, "I love you my sweet son,"

I know he really loved me and treated me like number one.

He was caring and gentle; I loved his laugh and smile,

He was the kind of person that if you asked him

To go a block, he would go a mile.

I'm sorry for the suffering, the anguish and pain,

But because of your cancer heaven did gain,

A wonderful, loving, dear Indian man

A guy that I miss like no other can.

I love you my precious father, I hope that you know

In heaven I will see you, my beloved, Indian Joe.

It was 1997 I've been married for four years now, and I am still madly in love with Judy and vice versa. I was taking a weekday evening course, and as the professor was talking, this next poem just came to me from out of nowhere. As he was talking, I was writing down the words like crazy. The professor must have thought I was taking great notes from his talk.

Pain In The World

God, why is there so much pain in the world?
Why did that man rape that innocent girl?
The poor little children that grow up abused
When they should be loved, they're treated like Jews.
The parents are neglectful, anger abounds
The kids are mistreated and thrown to the ground.
No one seems to care; there is no respect for life
The aged are tossed to the side or threatened with a knife.
Couples that should be loving and staying the course
Are calling it quits and ending in divorce.
Abandonment, alcoholism, depression, and drugs
Drive by shootings and people get mugged.
God I don't know why there is so much pain
But I'm glad that you sent Jesus to reign.
You love us so much, no matter how bad
When we turn to you, our life is made glad.
When I focus on the world it seems ugly and dim
It's depressing and discouraging and makes me feel grim.
But thank you dear God for giving real peace
In a world that is frightful and wars never cease.
Lord you give us love, esteem, worth and hope
In a crazy mixed up world, I know I can cope.

"And I heard a loud voice from the throne, saying, Behold, the tabernacle of God is among men, and He shall dwell among them, and they shall be His people, and God Himself shall be among them, and He shall wipe away every tear from their eyes; and there shall no longer be any death; there shall no longer be any mourning, or crying or pain; the first things have passed away"   Rev 21:3-4

Not too long after I wrote that poem, we made another important decision with lots of prayer behind it. I was going to stop going to seminary. A couple of reasons:

1) the professor in charge of the counseling department wanted me to change my major from M.Div. to MFCC (Marriage and Family Counselling) he thought I was great in that area. As it turned out, he was right. I have done lots of counseling over the years it's just something that God has given me to be able to really listen to people and know what they have been through or are going through and be able to help them. It helps since I have been through a lot over the years.

2) I ran out of money, and I needed to attend at least another year possibly more. It was a good decision, and I really enjoyed my time in seminary, but it just wasn't what I thought God wanted for me, and as you will see, I was right.

This next poem is another one that Judy wrote, and I thought it was beautiful.

A Morning Prayer

Help me O Lord this day

To follow you and your way

To be what you want for me

To conduct myself in your integrity

I'm only strong

When I'm not doing wrong

But striving to do what is right

With your life in me shinning bright

That only comes from doing your will

Listening to your voice and being still

That's what I want to do

As I commit this day to you

I could end my story and my poems right here, but I really feel like you need to hear what God has done with me over the years and how He has guided me into areas that I never would have dreamed I would do. I am not going to go into a lot of detail until I hit a spot that is quite amazing how God used me. There have been at least three or four times in my life when I said to God, "I don't deserve this God. You are too good to me."

I'm going to backtrack just a bit and go to 1995. In a few more years, I was going to be 50 (Yuck, that's old), or at least I thought so at the time. Anyway, I was at work and our complex hired some kids fresh out of college. I thought to myself, what do I have in common with these youngsters? I thought I should at least go and say hello. There was one in particular whose name was Karen, and she was a new graduate from UCLA. She was an amazing young person with a great sense of humor and personality. We hit it off like best buddies from the very beginning. Then there was another youngster who arrived a couple of months after Karen and his name was Mike and a new graduate from UC Davis. I met him, and again, we hit it off instantly. He loved to play tennis (I was better), and he also had a great sense of humor and personality.

I told you that I had a great ministry at work. I just loved to share with my workmates what was going on in my life and how God was helping me get through a really hard time. A good majority of the people I worked with came to our wedding. Speaking of weddings, I was asked to participate in a wedding with two of the people I worked with; the groom and I started Lockheed at the same time, and the bride was a very good friend of mine who helped me when I was going through my divorce. It was really great to be a part of their wedding. The sad thing is that I was also a big part of the bride's memorial service since she died of cancer.

To make a long story short (back to Mike and Karen), they fell in love and got married and I was also a part of their wedding, and I wrote a poem to read at the reception.

The Special Couple

From Lockheed Martin whence they came

I'm not sure exactly how it started or who to blame

What in common could these two provide?

From my point of view, how could they survive?

She was a graduate from UCLA

He was a graduate from north of the Bay

He is athletic from tennis to a hurdle

She can't even walk and her nickname is turtle

Lucky in gambling he wins all the time

She on the other hand can't even win a dime

What in common could these two provide?

From my point of view, how could they survive?

Ah, but then I focused on the inward heart

And what I discovered I should have seen from the start

Both are loving and generous and respectful and kind

None are quite like them, none you will find

They have a unique spirit that is so rare to see

They serve one another and not the selfish me

Where the one is weak the other is strong and bold

But the both have in common, hearts that are pure as gold

I think it is fortunate that I have such wonderful friends

Who I know will be together, forever till the very end.

We are still best friends, and they have helped Judy and me so much over the years. They are such a blessing, and I am so thankful that God brought them into my life.

It was 1999, and we were attending South Valley church in San Jose and there was a mission trip coming up that Judy and I wanted to go on. It was like no other mission trip I have ever been on or heard of. We were going to Rome, Italy, to pray. Pray for what you ask. The year 2000 was called the year of Jubilee and there would be thousands of Catholics coming to Rome from all over the world to celebrate and to get closer to God. Our mission was to walk all around Rome and pray for all the people who were coming to have a real spiritual awakening and get closer to God. It was amazing, walking around Rome and hitting all the main tourist places and praying that God would be glorified and that many Catholics would come to the Lord or renew their faith. I have an extremely close friend (Elena) who is Italian and lives in the Como area. I met her in 1986 when she came to England to stay with us and to learn English. She is Catholic but a very strong believer in Christ and always wants to know more about the bible. Judy and I went to England and Italy last year (2023) and visited all my friends in England and Elena and her family in Italy. Anyway, back to the Missions trip, two things happened that were worth mentioning.

(1) One day, we were all at the Parthenon and silently praying inside. One of the young ladies who was part of the church choir started to sing a hymn very softly. Before too long there were about six of us that started to sing with her but in a very soft tone. Then we heard someone (not part of our group) saying hush, so we thought we better

stop. Then we found out he didn't want us to stop but to hush the other people around us so he could hear our singing better. So we sang a little louder and everyone loved our singing the hymn, and God got the glory.

(2) Our last full day there we were all at a large square in Rome and again just praying for all the people coming to get closer to God. Any time you are doing something positive for God, guess who wants to interfere? The devil, the liar, was there to try and defeat us. As I was praying I looked up into the sky and started to see this big black cloud coming towards us. The closer it got I saw that it wasn't a cloud but a huge number of blackbirds coming. To me, it was like Satan coming to try and destroy our prayers and our work there. I started to pray for God to send those black birds away; just like Jesus when he cast out the demons from the possessed man from the Gerasenes (Luke 8:26-32). Before those ugly black birds got to the square, they veered off away from us, Praise God.

Now I'm going to jump to 2001. I was involved at church and still having a great time at work, plus I hit the 50 mark earlier. Back to the main story, I just felt that God wanted me to do something more than what I was doing, so one day, I went into my room at home, got down on my knees, and said, "God, I want to do more for you, I don't know what but I will do anything you want me to." The next day, I got a phone call from my work buddy Jim, and he said, "Hey, Gare, God said I should be in a bible study, and you should lead it." Talking about an answer to prayer, he said that he thinks there might be some others who might be interested also and he asked me to pray about it. I told him, "I already prayed about it, and yes, I will do it." Having a

Baptist background, I know that you should make the study 6-8 weeks long and about 90 minutes long, so we started on a Tuesday night at 6:30 or 7:00. There were just two that came the first night, and I found out that this was going to be a Catholic Bible study because everyone that attended at first was Catholic. It makes you wonder if this had anything to do with my previous story about our mission's trip to Rome to pray for the Catholics to get closer to God (I recently found out that one of the ladies who attended our bible study was in Rome during the Jubilee). I told them I only have one rule, and that is "you can ask anything you want at any time about the Bible." And Oh My Gosh, did they have tons of questions because Catholics don't study their bible? The first night turned into over two hours. We went from two people to three, then four, and it kept on growing. I decided that we would go over the book of Ephesians because it was short enough for me to cover in 8 weeks. At the end of the eight weeks, I assumed that we would stop, and that would be it – thank you very much. On the last night, one lady (Patricia) said, "Gary, I don't want to stop. Don't you love us?"

We continued to the end of 2001, and then they wanted more, so we continued until 2007, when Judy and I moved from the Bay area to Arizona. During that time frame, we got to as many as 25 people that attended, but in most cases we had 12 to 15. Most of the people who came attended St. Julie's Catholic church in San Jose, and the priest there (Father Jon) approved of our study. In fact, if someone from his congregation came to him and wanted to know about a bible study, he would send them to me. The other priest at St. Julie's church, Father Saju, actually attended the study for a few weeks. I guess to make sure

I wasn't teaching anything that was anti-Catholic, but all I was doing was going through a book of the Bible verse by verse, so he quit coming. Did anything else happen with this Bible study other than them learning more about God and getting closer to the Lord? Since you asked, the second wedding that I performed was with Ricardo (Ric) and Patricia, both from the Bible study. I was also a major part of another wedding from an individual who attended the Bible study (Clay and Tina). The only reason that I didn't perform the wedding was that Tina's father was a retired Judge, so he performed the ceremony but I did another portion. There was also another wedding from the Bible study (Adriana and Eugene). I love the Catholic people, and yes, they do some things differently than, say, the Baptist or non-denominational Christian churches, but there is only one thing that God wants in order to get into heaven, and that is found in John 14:6, and Jesus said, "I am the way the truth and the life. No one comes to the Father except through me." It doesn't say in scripture, "You aren't going to heaven unless you get baptized a certain way or you can't go to heaven if you don't speak in tongues (I had one old guy tell me that once). Acts 16:31 says, *"Believe on the Lord Jesus Christ and thou shalt be saved."* One thing I taught my Catholic friends was how to pray. I even took them out one night, and we did a prayer walk, and they loved it. My bible group is mighty when it comes to prayer, and they have spent a lot of time praying for me. I will tell you more about that later.

I had said earlier that Ric and Patricia was the second wedding that I performed, so who was the first? Funny you should ask (glad you are asking questions). I told you I had quite a ministry at work and that I was friends with almost everyone in my complex. There was this lady (Krista) who I worked with; very pretty, smart, and had a wonderful attitude with a love for food. We would go out to lunch quite a bit; she loved to try different foods, but she never ate that much. I would talk about Judy and what God was doing with me and about seminary, and she shared about her and her sister, and they bought a place in Los Gatos and just stuff in general. I also knew that she was dating Mateo, who also worked in our complex across the hall in the engineering section. I knew him quite well also. One day, Krista grabbed me and said let's go to lunch – no surprise. When we got there, she said I have something to tell you and ask you. She said, "Mateo and I want to get married, and we want you to do the wedding." I was speechless, but I told her I had gone to seminary, but I was not an ordained minister. She said, "You can do that online." Well, I said, "I would be honored to do your wedding, but I need to talk to my pastor first and see what he says." So, I talked to my pastor, who I knew very well, and told him that Krista wanted me to do the wedding and I told him about the online ordination thing. He said, "If you don't do it, then who will? Probably some other person who got ordained online." Then he said, "I will lend you my robe so you will look official. I actually got ordained in the church in 2005."

Since it was my first wedding, it took me longer to write up the ceremony, and it was a beautiful wedding and very God-centered. What a blessing for me and them. They will be celebrating their 20th anniversary this year (2024).

I have performed about 12-14 weddings over the years; all except one was to family or close friends. The last one was in December of 2023, when I was blessed to perform the wedding of my grandson.

Getting back to my Catholic Bible study for just a bit, here is another thing that happened because of one of the people who attended. His name was Clay; I mentioned him earlier because I was part of his wedding. Anyway, one day, he told me that he was a part-time teacher at a school for young kids who had trouble in regular high school. Clay was able to talk to one of the young ladies, and he told her about our Bible study and how much he enjoyed it. She said maybe you could come to where I live and do a Bible study. As it turned out she was staying at a place called "The Heritage Home." This place was part of San Jose City Team ministries and, at the time, was for young ladies who were pregnant and were going through a really hard time or had been abused. So Clay came to me and asked if we could go there sometime. We ended up going to the Heritage Home, and I did a Bible study at first just once a month, but the young ladies loved our study, and I did go a bit more and we did that for three or four years. I am still in contact with a couple of the ladies; another answer to prayer and a real blessing for the Heritage House girls and for our study. It taught them about God's love and compassion.

I am now going to jump ahead to March of 2006 because that was the year I went on a Missions trip to Ethiopia. I was attending Evergreen Valley Church, and my friend Sally was in charge of the group. There are a couple of things you need to know if you have never been on a missions trip: **1)** you will be blessed just as much if not more than the people that you are helping, and **2)** There is a good chance that things won't go exactly as you had planned, but when you put God first then it will go exactly as He wanted. We spent the first few days in the capital, Addis Ababa. While there, we helped to feed the homeless and needy and we all enjoyed that. Then we went north to Dese; the drive there was long but very beautiful. While at Dese we were working at a compound that had children from 6 years to 19 years old. We would help to teach in the classes, and in the afternoon, we would meet in a large building and talk to all the children from 12 to 19 years old. On one particular day, Ed and I were to speak to the kids; we had about 30 minutes, and we had to have an interpreter. At the last minute, Ed got sick, so I had to speak the entire time (no coincidence). I prayed that God would get the glory and the children would enjoy my talk. Before we got to Dese, we had stopped a couple of times and I observed a few things. I noticed that the Ethiopian children were very respectful to the elderly. I noticed that they were very family-oriented, and I noticed that even though they were very poor, they shared what they had. I have a Native American Indian heritage on my Father's side (Osage), which came in very handy. As I talked to the children, I put on a Native American T-shirt that I brought, and I told them about my heritage and how it is very much like there's. Then I told them about how God was also like that, how He loves all of us, and how He cares about the elderly and families. I don't remember a lot which is good because that means I spoke what God wanted me to and not what I had written down. Whatever I said, they were all (150) in tears, and then I prayed with them. When I left and went back to our bungalow shortly afterward, someone told me that the Ethiopian men in charge of the compound wanted to speak to me. My first thought was, *"Oh, no what did I say or do?"* It was just the opposite. They came to tell me that what I said touched their hearts like never before; he said these kids never cry. They are all used to death and he also said that a number of them accepted the Lord. Oh my! What an answer to prayer because God was definitely glorified and I felt so blessed.

It was 2007, the work that I was doing was moved to Colorado in 2005, and the facility was closing down so I moved from one site in Sunnyvale to another building not far away. I went from being the lead of all Mission Controllers on all shifts to being a Satellite test engineer, which I really loved. My plan was to work until I was 62, but Lockheed had other plans. There were a lot of layoffs that year, and I was one of them.

The big decision then was where do we go? We could not stay in the San Jose area because it was too expensive. I made a lot of money while I was working but not very much on retirement pay, and we had only purchased our house four years prior. Once or twice a year, we would travel out to Arizona and visit my daughter, who lived in Surprise, AZ. Each time we came out my daughter would always say, "Let me show you some houses." I had to leave my two Bible studies, the one at the Heritage Home and my Tuesday night Bible study. It was really hard, but there is more to come.

Judy and I ended up moving to Surprise, AZ, and we bought a house that we felt God really wanted us to have. It was November of 2007 when we moved in and the best thing was that just 5 miles away from the house was a brand new tennis facility that had 25 courts (I still play there). Before we left, Judy was complaining of pain in her stomach area, but the doctors said, "You have heartburn," and told her to take some Tums. Just before we actually left, my friend Karen wrote me a poem that I will share with you now.

A Friend Indeed

Congratulations to Gary Elliott, a friend indeed

Well, a different kind of friend, who loves to choke and tease you

Like it was his deed

When you first meet him, he politely says "Hi, my name is Gary."

But soon you find out he is something truly scary!

Strangely enough your teasing will truly be missed

Be assured though we'll think of you every time we are dissed.

So you're moving to Surprise, Arizona how appropriately named

How "surprised" your neighbors will be and even a little ashamed.

To meet their new neighbor who I named "The Chief"

They'll think, "At least there's that nice lady Judy. Fewh! What a relief.

So now you two lovebirds can spend countless hours together

I'm sorry Judy. Just get some earplugs; you won't even hear

The drop of a feather

To our friend we say, "A goodbye this is not."

Maybe we'll visit you in Arizona when it's not so dang hot!

We all love you very much with your heart of gold

Our friendships will always stay strong and never grow old

We have all been blessed that you have crossed our paths

We appreciate your kindness, generosity and the endless amount of laughs

You ae a true friend that always helps anyone in need

Best wishes to Gary, to the greatest friend indeed.

We were settling down in our new home with a nice swimming pool in the backyard for those hot sunny days that were to come. It was 2008 and it had dawned on me that I forgot to mention a family member that was very important to us. Her name was Miso. She was a Dalmatian mix that we got secondhand. Judy's son had her along with another dog, but when he had to move to the new place they said, "You can have one dog only." So he said, "Mom, will you watch Miso until I find someone else?" That is how we got Miso but she was a wonderful dog and lived to be 17; I still miss her.

One day, Judy was taking the dog for a walk, and when she got back, she said, "I'm really tired." We just thought it was the heat since we were not used to the Arizona heat. This went on for a couple of weeks, and each time Judy took the dog out, she came back sooner, and finally, she only lasted 50 feet. We thought we better see a doctor. At that time, we were going to Luke AFB for our medical help, so we made an appointment for Judy to see a doctor.

He said, "I think you need to see a cardiologist, and if you have any more instances where you feel bad, you should call 911."

We made an appointment to see a cardiologist, and we didn't have to wait that long to see him. That weekend, we decided to go to the local mall. We got there and started to walk to the entrance, which wasn't that far, but before we got there, Judy said," I don't feel good, I can't make it to the entrance."

I said, "Should we call 911?"

She said, "I don't know, what do you think?"

We decided not to call, and it is amazing to me how God protects us in our ignorance. He always cares for and about His children. Within a couple of days, we went to see the cardiologist, and we thought they would run some tests and prescribe some medication, and that would be that. The first thing they did was give Judy an EKG, and it was fine. Then we saw the doctor, and he asked some questions. Judy told him how when she took the dog out for a walk, she couldn't walk very far before she got exhausted. Then he said something that we were not expecting, "You are not going home; you are going straight to the hospital, and tomorrow we will do an angiogram." We were somewhat in shock, but we followed his orders. The hospital was very close by. The next day, Judy had her angiogram, and they came back and said something even more shocking, "We found out that you have one artery that is 99% blocked, and we could not get past it to give you a stent, so you will have open-heart surgery tomorrow." What! Are you kidding me? I am crying just writing this down. We had family in town and told them immediately, along with Judy's sons, my sister, and Mike and Karen. My Aunt and Uncle lived very close to us, and they were there along with my daughter the next day to pray with me. Lots of others were praying for Judy, especially the old Tuesday night Bible study group and lots of friends at my old work. They told Judy who her surgeon would be and what time she would be having the surgery. The next day (surgery day), they came to tell us that her surgeon would not make it because he was having surgery in Scottsdale, and there were complications, and he wouldn't make it back in time.

Then they told Judy, "You can either wait until tomorrow to have him do the surgery, or you can have Dr. Kathuria today."

I told the nurse, "Please give us a minute. We need to pray about this."

She closed the curtain, and I started to pray; I hadn't got more than a couple of words out when all of a sudden, the curtain came flying open, and a nurse jumped on the bed and said, "I heard that you might get Dr. Kathuria?" Then she went on to say, "He is the head of the department and our best surgeon and he did my father's open-heart surgery."

Talk about an answer to prayer and I hadn't even finished the prayer. Judy had her surgery; it was a double bypass, and she had some complications, but Dr. Kathuria had no problems because he is the best. So much for the heartburn they told us Judy had in San Jose. From what I have learned, this is a common issue with women. They don't have the same symptoms that men have. It has been 15 years, and Judy is fine; she just had a checkup, and the same cardiologist who sent us to the hospital said she is doing really well. This also shows you how important the power of prayer is, and I am so thankful for all the prayer warriors that I have out there.

It was the middle of June, and it is almost Father's Day and I really felt the need to write a poem dedicated to my Lord and Father. I don't remember if my kids did anything for me this particular year, but in years to come, they made up for it. My kids really love me, especially my daughter. They are all amazing and I am so proud of them and blessed to have such wonderful children who truly love their father.

Father

I have a loving Father who truly cares for me
He watches and He listens, oh so tenderly.
He never breaks a promise; His word is straight and true
He promises to never leave me, to make me brand new.
When I cry, or when I'm hurting and in pain
He comes close to me in love, and tells me it's for my gain.
My Father hates to see me wander, to be selfish or stray
But he stands with his arms wide open and to me he does say,
"I love you my precious, please don't go away."
He loves to spend time with me, to show me what's right
No matter where I go, or where I roam I'm always in his sight.
My Father never yells or screams or loses His control
He's full of love and patience and wants to make me whole.
When I'm tired and weary and feel I can't go on
He strengthens and encourages and whispers, "This is my beloved
son."
My Father doesn't spoil me with worldly things that waste and fade
away
He gives me all His love, joy and grace to rise above the difficulties
And help others along the way.
His discipline is never harsh; it's always what I need
To make me more like Him, who is perfect indeed
Oh, I really love my Father, I guess you can see
I love to call Him "Abba" because He is Heavenly.

Well, I would love to say I have escaped any serious health issues, but that is not quite the truth. I won't go into a lot of detail (just yet), but here are a couple of highlights. I am a fitness fanatic and have been a gym rat since I was 17. I was very athletic when I was young before I knew it was popular. Since I grew up in San Diego close to the beach (Mission Beach and Pacific Beach), I used to run up and down the beach just for fun, and I rode my bike a lot and even had a paper route. When I got to High School I was on the varsity tennis team and football. When I went into the Air Force, I played a lot of tennis and racquetball, and when I started working at Lockheed, I started to do weight training (I got to do 305lbs on the bench press).

One day, Judy and I were visiting San Jose (2009), and I went to the gym. I was doing the bench press, and on the way up, I heard and felt a pop in my right shoulder. When we got back to Arizona, I saw the orthopedic doctor at Luke AFB, and he told me I had torn my rotator cuff, the labrum, and a partial tear of the bicep. Needless to say, I needed and got surgery for that, and all went well. The physical therapy was grueling but successful, and back to tennis.

Moving along to 2011, I went to see a urologist since my doctor in San Jose said that my PSA was a bit elevated. This doctor said that my PSA had gone up considerably and I should get a biopsy, and after having two biopsies, they told me I had prostate cancer. It didn't seem to bother me or phase me at all because I was actually expecting it. I went through 9 weeks of radiation and kept playing tennis through it, and all was good. Again, the power of prayer was amazing. It has been 13 years, and my PSA is still at zero.

So much for the medical stuff, at least for a while. What was I doing on the spiritual side of the house? I have mentioned a few times now how important it is to listen to God, and when you are close to Him, it is easy to hear God. I was actually going to leave this next portion out, but I felt that it was really important and it is a great example of listening to God. I was driving down the road one day, and out of nowhere, I distinctly heard God say to me, *"Call Dennis Hollenbeck."* He is an old high school buddy of mine, and it was kind of weird that I heard God speak to me so clearly. I pulled over so I could call him; usually, when you call someone, they answer the phone with "hello", or they might even say, "Hey Gary how's it going?" But the first words out of his mouth were, "My daughter is dead." How do you respond to something like that? I don't know exactly what I said except, "I am so sorry, blah, blah, blah, and I am here for you my friend." I put the blah, blah, blah in because I don't know exactly what I said; it was all God telling me what to say. The conversation was short because he was in the car just leaving the hospital, and then we hung up. I was in shock, and all I could do was start to pray for him and his wife (she was in the car as well) and his family. I decided to call Dennis later that evening, knowing that he would not answer the phone because he would be too busy calling family or them calling him, so I would just leave a message to try and encourage him. When I called, he actually answered the phone, and he said, "Thank you for calling us earlier. What you said was exactly what we needed." We talked for just a bit, and I found out that his daughter had committed suicide, and I again spoke whatever God gave me to say. It was a couple of months later when I heard God say to call my same friend again. This time, I hesitated, thinking I was pretty sure I heard God, but maybe I didn't, so I waited a day to call. I called the next day, and this time, his first words were, "My wife and I thought you were going to call yesterday because my mother passed away." I apologized and told him that God told me to call yesterday, but I didn't do what God told me to do. I would have never heard God speak to me if I wasn't close to God and listening. In scripture, a good example is the Apostle John; he was the listener, and he was the closest (physically) to God. Jesus had his twelve Apostles, but three were the very closest (Peter, James, and John). They were with him at the Mount of Transfiguration, and John was the one closest to Jesus at the Last Supper. Also, in John, during the arrest of Jesus in the garden of Gethsemane, Peter cuts off the ear of the servant named Malchus **(John 18:10).** The servant's name is only mentioned in the book of John and nowhere else in scripture. Why? Because John was the closest to Jesus and the only one who could hear what his name was. Come close to God and He will come close to you **(James 4:8).**

It took us a little while to find the right church, but we finally settled down at Calvary Chapel Surprise. One of the first things I asked the senior pastor was, "Do you have a prison ministry?" because I really felt that God wanted me to do that. The answer was "No." We did get involved in a Bible study, and I was able to teach once in a while. I also got involved in the prayer ministry and the hospital visitation ministry.

In 2012, I was talking to a friend of ours who also went to Calvary Chapel and he was telling me about the prison ministry that he was doing with another friend of his. I said, "Prison ministry, I was told there wasn't one." He said he had just started it; he and his friend were both retired prison correctional officers in Northern California. I told him I wanted to get involved, and he said there was a process, but he wanted more guys to get involved. It was nothing for me to get the clearance, and before long I was going out to Lewis Prison in Buckeye, AZ. There are two different sides to Lewis Prison. On one side (east of Highway 85) are the inmates who are there for a short time and have a lot of freedom. On the other side (west of Highway 85) is the main facility and it ranges from Low to High security. I was trained at the east side with minimum security. Once I was trained, I was given a place to start my Bible study. Since I had never done prison ministry before, I expected they would put me in a minimum or low-security facility. God had other plans for me; they told me I would be on the west side at the Morey unit, the blue side. I looked it up on the internet, and it said high security, and they had a riot there two years previous. Needless to say, I was scared to death, but you know what God says about being afraid or scared? Do not be afraid for I am with you (**John 6:20**). I didn't know how many would come, if they would be in chains, or if a guard would be with them. It was about a 50-minute drive from my house to the prison, and I prayed all the way. I even called a friend and asked him to pray for me. God had me covered because when I got there, they were not prepared for me; the Chaplain had not sent down the paperwork that the guards needed to get the inmates out of their cells to attend the bible study. Next week was another story; they were ready for me, and the inmates came in with a guard, and they were not chained. I believe I had about 12 to 15 inmates, and most of the time, I had about 15 to 20 inmates. I told them from the very beginning that I did not want to know why

84

they were in prison. I was at Morey for 4 and a half years, and it was an amazing experience. They loved the Bible study, and they loved me. One thing that really stood out for me was that every week at the end of the study when they had to go back to their cells, they always thanked me for being there and for what they had learned. I must admit there were a couple of guys that, before I could say no, shared why they were there, and both said they were in for murder, but it didn't seem to affect me other than feel sorry for them and love them a little more. When I first started, I had the inmates sitting in a circle or sometimes sitting at the tables. There was one inmate who at first sat by himself and not with the group. Later on, I found out his nickname was Thumper (not the bunny in Bambi). He was called Thumper because he was the enforcer, and no one messed with him or me because if they did, he was all over them. We became best friends after a while, and I really miss him. I had one other young man who attended only for a short while, but I was amazed at how polite he was, how knowledgeable he was of the Bible, and how humble he was. Again, he shared with me not why he was in prison but how long his sentence was. When he told me he was in for 65 years, I knew it was more than just a drug bust or petty theft. He wasn't there long because they moved him over to the red side of Morey. Another thing I wanted to mention was that after about 4-6 months the guard quit coming in with the inmates and staying with us. They trusted me a lot, and they trusted the inmates. During my time there, some inmates accepted Christ into their lives, and a lot of them came closer to God and recommitted their lives to the Lord. I was at Lewis Prison from March 2012 to August 2016. There was a reason I stopped in 2016, which I will explain later, plus another miracle at prison.

Not only did I have a great ministry at the prison, but it spilled over to my regular life. I played tennis with a bunch of guys who were about my age and my skill level, and on Fridays, they would always ask, "What are you doing this weekend?" My response would always be "I'm going to prison." I would get the strangest looks until I told them I was a chaplain at Lewis prison and I did a Bible study on Saturday nights. That was a great witnessing tool. They all knew I was an ordained minister and respected me for doing what I was doing at the prison. One day, one of my tennis buddies came to me and asked if I would do a memorial service for his wife, who had recently passed away from cancer, and I was more than happy to do that.

I also had a bible study going on at my house that met every Tuesday except the last Tuesday we took off so I could refresh and get ready for the next month. We had a lot of people come and go; some moved away, some went to another church, and a few stayed for a very long time. One time my friend Richard brought a friend by the name of Adrian. He loved coming to our Bible study, and he would say, "This is my church, and you are my family." He lived by himself, and he was just getting by. Many times, we would give him food to take home, and he really appreciated it. His health was not very good; he had a lot of medical issues. As you all know, COVID-19 came in 2019/2020. We had our end-of-year bible study in early December 2020, but Adrian did not come because Richard said that he was not well. Richard said that we should take him some food the next day where he was staying, so we did. When he finally answered the door, we could tell he was not well at all. We gave him the food, prayed with him, and then left. A day or two later, I got a call from his landlord saying that Adrian was in the hospital because he passed out in the bathroom and I should come over and get his wallet and things to take to the hospital. I went over and went through his room, touched everything, found the items he wanted or needed and took it to the hospital. About a week or two later, Judy and I were not feeling well, so we went to Urgent Care at the hospital. They tested us and took our temperature and oxygen levels. We were both okay, so they sent us home. A few days later I told Judy I feel worse and I know I have a temperature. When I went back, I had a temperature of 101, and my oxygen level was 85%, so they told me I was going to be admitted to the hospital, this was on January 1, 2021. There were a lot of people in the hospital with COVID-19, and I had to wait 5 hours before they gave me a room. And as God would have it, I was in the bed next to Adrian. What a coincidence – not. That is one thing I preach all the time: there are no coincidences; read the book of Esther. I was able to talk to Adrian and pray for him and with him. His doctor came in and said that he needed to have something special done, but he needed to check with Adrian's pastor and guardian. Adrian said, "He is in the bed next to me." I didn't know that he had put me in charge of his medical decisions. The doctor told me that Adrian was in pretty bad shape, not only because of COVID-19 but because of his heart, diabetes, and other things. I was only in the hospital for five days and was released, but Adrian was still there. I prayed with him before I left. It was only a few days later that the hospital called me to say that he had passed away. I know that he is with the Lord, and he has no more pain or tears.

I am now going back to 2016; I was still going to Luke AFB for my medical issues. The doctor, for the past year or so, kept saying, "Your blood test doesn't seem quite right; we will check it again later and see if it changes." This went on for a year, then one day, I saw a different doctor, and he said almost the same thing with one exception. He said, "Your blood test doesn't look right. I think you need to see a hematologist." He said I know a couple of doctors. You could see one of them or anybody else you wish to see. I made an appointment to see Dr. Singh at the Arizona Center for Cancer Care (AZCCC). He looked at my blood test and ran a blood test as well. Later on, he told me, "I don't think you have Multiple Myeloma, but it is best if I do the following test: a bone marrow biopsy, x-rays to look at your bones to see how strong they are, and a more thorough blood test." The x-rays were easy, and they must have done at least 12-15 of them. The blood tests were a breeze, but the bone marrow biopsy was the most painful thing I have ever experienced. I was supposed to see Dr. Singh on a certain date, but they called me and said that he wanted to see me sooner. Judy had a Bible study that day, and I told her to go ahead and go. I'm sure everything is fine. I got there and went in to talk to the doctor and his assistant. I remember he said, "You have Multiple Myeloma and blah, blah, blah," because I was in shock when he said I had cancer and didn't hear a thing after that. He was telling me what was going to happen next, but it was all a blur. I wanted to say, "Stop, let me get my wife," but I was speechless. When I left his office, I wanted to call Judy, but I knew she was still in her Bible study and could not be reached, so I called my daughter Eryn. I only said a word or two and she said I will be right over to your house. She stayed with me and cried until Judy got home, and then we all cried. I was taking chemo from July 2016 until December 2016, and then I was supposed to have a transplant in Scottsdale. Before I go any further, and there is more, I want to share this poem that I wrote concerning my cancer.

Cancer Poem
(2016)

*No, no, no this can't be true I'm not ready for this look what you're
going to put me through*

*I had nine weeks of radiation for prostate and lost my mom and dad,
I hate this cancer stuff it really makes me mad*

Are you sure you have the right person, could the test be wrong?

*I'm in really good shape, play tennis, go to the gym I think I'm
pretty strong.*

*Now you are telling me I have to go through three months of chemo
following that I have a transplant and a fair chance of living?*

*But Lord I've been faithful, serving, loving, a good person and
giving.*

I just can't believe it; I know I'm in shock

*My wife and family really need me I'm not ready to punch out my
clock.*

*As time goes by and I start to realize after many days and nights
with tears in my eyes*

*That no matter what happens my Lord is still King and He will bring
me through this illness and lots of other things.*

*As time goes by this cancer is not fun and at times makes me sick but
as long as I keep my focus on God I will not quit*

*I have so many family and friends that love me so dear, they
encourage me with prayer, calls, emails and all*

*Thank you Lord it's you that gets the glory I know when I'm done I
will have a wonderful story*

90

I was only scheduled to have 3 months of chemo and then have an autologous stem cell transplant, but it took 5 months, and here is the reason it lasted longer than it was supposed to. Judy was told she needed to have a mammogram. She didn't want to, but she did. They called her and said you need to come back because we think there might be something there. As it turned out, she did have breast cancer, but they caught it really early. She ended up getting a mastectomy and had seven weeks of radiation. She has been cancer-free free 6 years now. Again, that is due to the power of prayer that they found her cancer so early. We had so many people praying for me, and for her, it was unbelievable.

That was the reason for my delay in getting my transplant because they didn't want me to get my transplant until she had her mastectomy and was in the clear; otherwise, they thought it would have been too stressful for me. So, in December, I had my transplant. I was in the hospital only for a couple of days, and I did lose my hair (for a while). The doctor in charge of my transplant said, "It will take 90 days before you will be better." Again, because of the power of prayer and my good health, I was better in 30 days, which was way faster than most everyone. It did take me quite a while to get my strength and stamina back but I was on the tennis court in no time. The one thing about Multiple Myeloma, though, is that they will tell you "it will come back." The average at the time was 3 -5 years, but it can be a lot longer. That is why I had to stop my Bible study at Morey because of my cancer.

Once I felt well enough, I started my home Bible study again, and I felt the urge to go back to Lewis prison so I did in March of 2018 for one year. This time, I was on the west side at Sunrise. This was a low-security area and the inmates just came by themselves with no guards. I had a good turnout at first, but after a while, not too many came because they moved a bunch of the guys to a different facility because they worked outside the prison.

One other amazing thing happened that was related to Lewis prison. One day, I got a Facebook message asking if I was the same Gary Elliott, who was a chaplain at Lewis prison, and the person asking was a young lady named Angelina. I wrote back and told her I was, and we agreed to meet. Judy and I met her and she was very pretty and extremely nice and pleasant. She told me a story that was unbelievable and straight from God. She said that she was engaged to an inmate at Lewis prison who remembered me. He was at Morey for a while, and one day, the guard came to get him to go to the Bible study. He told the guard that he had not signed up to go, but the guard insisted that he go. He came to the study and said he loved it and kept coming back. All he remembered when he talked to Angelina was there was a guy who led the Bible study, and his name was Gary Elliott and he was a tennis player. She was able to find me on Facebook. They wanted to get married and thought of me. It is pretty rare that the prison allows an inmate to get married while still in prison, but because I had been there as a chaplain, they allowed it. In November 2019, I performed the wedding of Will and Angelina. Angelina attended my Bible study for a good while, and Will finally got released in 2022.

I had mentioned some time ago I would tell you more about my Catholic Bible study. Almost as soon as I left San Jose and got settled in Arizona, my old Bible study wanted to start the Bible study back up, but we just couldn't figure out a way to do that. Plus, I was too busy with Judy. I believe it was 2018 when we finally figured out how to get the old study back together again (Zoom). From the old group, we had eight, plus Elena from Italy and Judy and myself. We had a great time together studying the word, and always, at the end, we would pray. When I found out that my cancer came back (next paragraph), they were the first to pray for me. On one occasion, when I couldn't meet with them, they got together and just spent the evening praying for me. I have to tell you, and I am being 100% honest here, there were times coming up when I could actually feel the prayers for me; it was amazing.

I was going to AZCCC for a blood test every month to check on my cancer status. It was April 28th 2021, and I found out that my cancer had come back, so I had to have another bone marrow biopsy, but this time I went to the hospital to get really numbed up. For the next 2 years, I went through all the old chemo drugs and some of the new drugs, and they either didn't work from the beginning or they worked for a few months and quit working. I remember one especially because it caused me the most pain and misery. I would start getting terrible shakes at first, not too bad, but it kept getting worse quickly. And I would also get a temperature of 100 or a little more, and I would get the chills. Finally, they said we don't have anything else to give you. As it turns out (no coincidence), there was an opening that just came up for a clinical trial in Scottsdale with a world-famous doctor (Dr. Mikhael); he is one of the top three doctors in the world who only deals with Multiple Myeloma. I started the clinical trial in July 2023, and it looked good at first, but eventually, it did not work. We already had plan B lined up and that was a fairly new program that had only been approved by the FDA a year and a half. It is called CAR T-cell therapy. They take out your T-cells send them off to a manufacturing facility and they clean them up and add something to them; send the T-cells back and put them into me. Dr. Abraham Kanate was in charge of this procedure. So in November of 2023, I had to have three straight days of chemo, and then they put the T-cells in me, and I had to spend eleven days in the hospital. The first two days were rough, but after that, not too bad. I was very happy to get released and go home. Because of the drugs and transplant, I was not allowed to drive for 60 days, so poor Judy had to do all the driving. About a month after my release from the hospital, they had to do another bone marrow biopsy and major blood test to see if the new T-cells were working. It was a real miracle indeed; I could not believe how fast and how far my numbers came down. There is one particular test run that tells me how my Myeloma is doing. It is called the IGG Kappa Light Chain and it was over 1,000; normal should be less than 70. When I got the results and saw the Light Chain number, I was shocked because it was 3. On January 29, 2024 Dr. Kanate told me I had no more cancer cells; the words I had been waiting to hear for over 2 years, but he said that there was still an issue, and that was my M-Spike number was elevated. All I know is that I owe all the praise and glory to God and all the thanks to my family and friends (all over the world) who prayed and are still praying for me. Without them, I may not have made it. Just remember, "You can get through this with God's help."

I want to thank all of you for reading my book, traveling with me through the years, and seeing how much God has been with me and Judy and is still using me for His glory.

Made in the USA
Monee, IL
03 October 2024

67110230R00059